Blinded by the Light

Ann M Thomas

Alina Publishing
Swansea

Published by Alina Publishing
45 Rhondda Street, Mount Pleasant
Swansea SA1 6ER

ISBN: 978-1-9996781-4-2

Printed by Kindle Print

Available from Amazon
Will also available on Amazon for Kindle and
Smashwords.com for multiple ebook formats

Cover design by Steve Jones

About the Author:

Ann M Thomas joined The Church of Jesus Christ of Latter Day Saints at the age of 16 along with her family. She met and married her husband Michael, had 4 children and served in that church in many ways before she and Michael realised their error and found the truth. They were saved in 1986, but their experience has given them an insight into Christian cults and cultic thinking.

Writing poetry and making up stories since she was a child, she only started to write seriously when her children were grown. Her main ambition was to write science fiction, but along the way she got fascinated by local history and distracted by a major stroke. However, she wrote poetry about her stroke and spent her recovery writing a local history book. Taking early retirement gave her more time to concentrate on her writing.

Connect with the author online:
Website: https://www.annmariethomas.co.uk
Email: amt.tetelestai@gmail.com
Twitter: https://twitter.com/AnnMThomas80
Facebook: http://on.fb.me/1P9OkCu
Amazon: http://amzn.to/1EjoBAZ
LinkedIn: http://linkd.in/1MUdsAv
GoodReads: http://bit.ly/21nG4Jv

FREE BOOK!
Join the author's mailing list and receive these free
books and monthly updates http://eepurl.com/bbOsyz

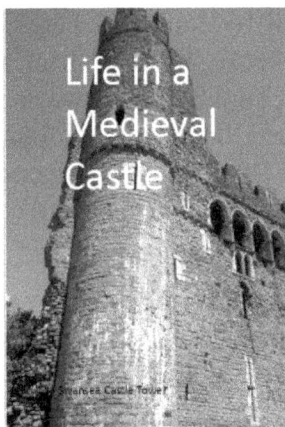

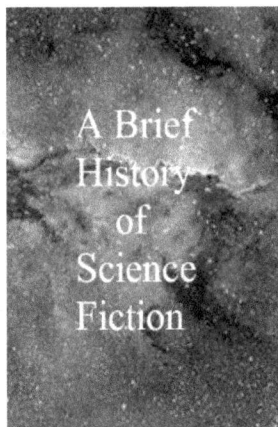

TABLE OF CONTENTS

INTRODUCTION

In my search for God I got diverted into error: I found the Mormon* Church. They were a lovely group of people and very sincere, but they were wrong. It took me eighteen years to realise that they weren't teaching the true gospel. When I finally became a true Christian I realised how subtle the error was. Not blatantly opposed to the truth but subtle changes that were hard to spot. And taught by such nice people, sincere people, many of whom were deceived themselves.

In the many years since then I have noticed how the same errors can creep into the church. Secure in the belief that they are saved and taught by sincere and nice people, Christians can slip into error almost unnoticed. We must be on our guard. This little book is here to help you.

> *But you are a chosen people, a royal priesthood, a holy nation, a people belonging to God, that you may declare the praises of him who called you out of darkness into his wonderful light. (1 Peter 2:9)*

These are uplifting, glorious words. We are so grateful, as Christians, to be in that position. We look with sympathy on those people in the Christian cults who are deceived, such as Mormons* and Jehovah's Witnesses. No matter how sincere their desire to serve God, they have been deceived by false doctrines. Christians believe, quite rightly, that we are in the light and those people in the cults are in the dark.

I remember being challenged by a Mormon* missionary over Romans 10:9:

> If you declare with your mouth, "Jesus is Lord," and believe in your heart that God raised him from the dead, you will be saved.

He said he believed and declared to me then and there 'Jesus is Lord,' so by that definition he was saved. This was a puzzle, because I knew from past experience that Mormons aren't saved as Evangelical Christians understand 'saved', so what about this Scripture? The answer took some thinking about, but then I realised that the Mormon Church teaches a different Jesus.

Their Jesus is the brother of Satan and was conceived through actual intercourse between Mary and God the Father, who is an exalted man and has a physical body. There are many other errors in their theology, including their belief that Jesus paid for our sins in Gethsemane, not on the cross. So belief and confession aren't necessarily the same. You have to make sure you have the right Jesus, that your confession reflects not just your personal beliefs, but biblical truth.

Unfortunately, the security Christians feel in being in

the light can make us complacent and blind to the fact that we are prey to many of the same errors found in the cults. If we don't study the Scriptures and nurture our relationship with God, we too can find ourselves confused, misled, and wandering away from the truth. Let me give you another, more sobering Scripture than the one we began with:

> *You, therefore, have no excuse, you who pass judgement on someone else, for at whatever point you judge the other, you are condemning yourself, because you who pass judgement do the same things. (Romans 2:1)*

The message of salvation is clear, there can be no mistake. The only way to God is through Jesus Christ and his sacrifice. We can't merit anything by our own efforts, but must lean on the grace of God, which gives us what we don't deserve, and saves us from what we do deserve. This doesn't make sense to the fallen human mind.

> *There is a way that seems right to a man, but in the end it leads to death. (Prov.14:12)*

We need to change our perspective, and look at things from God's point of view, before we can understand. But even after we've accepted Christ, the 'old man' (2 Cor.5:17) keeps intruding and we can easily lose sight of him again.

James tells us that the word of God is like a mirror that shows us who we really are and where we stand. We were saved because we looked into that mirror, saw the truth, and acted on that truth. Yet as soon as we go away from the mirror, we forget what we look like. We forget we were reconciled to God through the finished work of Jesus, not our own efforts. We look for things to do to put us right with God, or to make our Christian lives more effective.

> *Anyone who listens to the word but does not do what it says is like a man who looks at his face in a mirror and, after looking at himself, goes away and immediately forgets what he looks like. But the man who looks into the perfect law that gives freedom, and continues to do this, not forgetting what he has heard, but doing it--he will be blessed in what he does. (James 1:23-25)*

We've grasped the perfect law that gives freedom, and we need to hold on to it and enjoy its blessings. But for every truth there is a trap, a subtle distortion of truth, into which we can fall. Unless we're aware of these traps and are on our guard, we can find we're losing that joy and peace we knew when we were first saved. Satan is cunning. We're watching for wickedness and evil traps, so he works in subtler ways. Little by little, when we don't realise, he'll lead us away and rob us.

The Psalmist pleaded with God: *"Restore to me the joy of your salvation" (Ps.51:12)*, and the Lord condemned the church in Ephesus: *"You have forsaken your first love" (Rev.2:4)*. I'm sure they didn't callously and deliberately turn their backs on God. Indeed, they are praised in the preceding verses. But somewhere along the way, they forgot.

In the following sections we'll look at some of the traps into which we can fall. Each of these is a distortion of the truth, so we'll look at the truth, the trap, and the solution to the problem. It's my prayer that you'll be able to recognise where you may have been deceived, and may be helped back to the truth of the '*perfect law that gives freedom.*'

- - - - -

*The Church of Jesus Christ of Latter-day Saints no longer likes to be called Mormon, but The Church of Jesus Christ. This is part of their move to be recognised as a Christian denomination, which they are not.

LEGALISM

The Truth

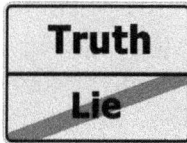

For it is by grace you have been saved through faith--and this not from yourselves, it is the gift of God--not by works, so that no-one can boast. (Eph. 2:8)

We need to realise there's absolutely nothing we can do to save ourselves. If God had not freely given us salvation, we'd have been forever lost. We grasp hold of salvation simply by believing it's possible, and by accepting the sacrifice of Christ on our behalf.

God puts no conditions on this. He doesn't require a certain form of behaviour or level of good works before he justifies us. We come as we are, good or bad. The important thing is that we come, and believe.

> *When you were dead in your sins and in the uncircumcision of your sinful nature, God made you alive with Christ. (Col. 2:13-15)*

Having been saved, we can take no credit. God did it without reference and without response from us. We were not even consulted when the plan was formulated, and Jesus came to die for us. God's love overflowed to us when we were far away and he did what was necessary to bring us back.

> *Once you were alienated from God and were enemies in your minds because of your evil behaviour. But now he has reconciled you by Christ's physical body through death to present you holy in his sight, without blemish and free from accusation. (Col.1:21-22)*

God, the Almighty Eternal God, declares all those who have believed to be completely and absolutely righteous in his sight. God is willing to say, over each one of us, however bad we've been, however hard we've tried, that we are righteous in his sight now and for ever, whatever the future holds.

The Trap

Legalism is the disease that paralyses Christians who fall short of living in the reality of the new life.

The theory is wonderful, but the practicalities of daily living can be something else. You want to be the best you can be for God. You want to make a difference where you live, where you work, where you are. You really want to know that presence of the kingdom coming out of your life that makes a difference to the people around you. You want to move into the fullness of what God has called you to.

But so often you feel powerless, impotent, ineffective, weak. Faced with the cycle of failure and uphill struggling, you apply the wrong medicine: I'll try harder, I'll pray more, I'll go to prayer meeting, I'll get involved, I'll understand the Bible, I'll get serious about me and God, I'll do more things.

'What has happened to all your joy?' (Gal.4:15).

This applies to you when legalism is getting a grip in your life. Your joy disappears. Anyone who adds anything to the pure gospel of Jesus Christ actually takes away from it, and when we try to add our own efforts we end up losing touch with God. Eternal life is a gift, and it's an insult to the giver to attempt to pay for it.

> *You who are trying to be justified by law have been alienated from Christ; you have fallen away from grace. (Gal.5:4)*

Falling from grace is returning to a system of religious

observance to keep God happy. It comes into all our lives. It's subtle, and it catches you unawares.

> *Did you receive the Spirit by observing the law, or by believing what you heard? Are you now so foolish? After beginning with the Spirit, are you now trying to attain your goal by human effort?... Does God give you his Spirit and work miracles among you because you observe the law, or because you believe what you heard?...Christ redeemed us from the curse of the law by becoming a curse for us,... so that by faith we might receive the promise of the Spirit. (Gal.3:2, 3, 5, 13, 14).*

It was not just the Galatians who fell into this trap. There's probably not a Christian on earth who has not at some time found themselves '*now trying to attain your goal by human effort.*'

The Solution

We've already quoted James' comment about the word of God being a mirror *(James 1:23-25)*. We need to go back continuously to look in that mirror. We need to remind ourselves who we are and where we stand in Christ, so we will not forget. Paul urged the Galatians:

It is for freedom then that Christ has set us free. Stand firm, then, and do not let yourselves be burdened again by a yoke of slavery. (Gal.5:1)

Paul qualified for worthiness, if anyone did, by the works he did. He described himself as *'a Hebrew of Hebrews'* and *'as for legalistic righteousness, faultless.' (Philip.3:3,5)* And yet, once he discovered grace, he realised it was all worthless.

I consider them rubbish, that I may gain Christ and be found in him, not having a righteousness of my own that comes from the law, but that which is through faith in Christ. (Philip.3:8-9)

James talked about faith and deeds, but put them in the right perspective:

What good is it, my brothers, if a man claims to have faith but has no deeds? Can such faith save him? (James 2:14)

The kind of faith which saves, is the kind that produces the deeds. In other words, the things you do are the result of your faith, not the cause of it. We should remember that *'God looks on the heart' (1 Sam.16:7)*. He doesn't need us to prove anything to him.

If we are bound up in 'doing the right things,' it's not the things we do that need to change, but our attitude. We need to understand with our hearts and not just our heads. For example:

- We have *'every spiritual blessing in Christ'.*
- We are *'holy and blameless in his sight'.*
- We are *'adopted as his sons'.*
- We have *'redemption through his blood, the forgiveness of sins, in accordance with the riches of God's grace that he lavished on us.'*
- The Holy Spirit is *'a deposit guaranteeing our inheritance.'*

(Eph.1:3-14)

There is an old saying: *'There is nothing you can do to make God love you any more, and there is nothing you can do that will make God love you any less*.'

Try reading Ephesians, Galatians, and Romans chapters 6, 7 & 8. And then act on that!

MAGIC FORMULAS

The Truth

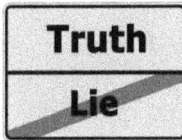

He who did not spare his own Son, but gave him up for us all – how will he not also, along with him, graciously give us all things? (Rom.8:32)

One of the hardest things in Christian life is reconciling our desires with what God wants for our lives. He knows us, he knows what is best for us, and he has a part for us to play in his plan. We know what we want. We learn very quickly in our Christian life to pray and ask God for his blessings, but we also need to learn to wait on his time and accept his will.

There is no 'magic' way to move God. He is sovereign and cannot be coerced or persuaded. If our appeals to him directly appear to receive no response, there is no other way. The only exception to this is when there is something wrong in our lives which has affected our standing before God, and this needs to be put right. This is no magic formula, just a re-establishing of our relationship on the right footing.

The Trap

1. *When you ask, you do not receive, because you ask with wrong motives... Wash your hands, you sinners, and purify your hearts, you double minded. (James 4:3,8)*

It is true that sometimes prayers are not answered and blessings not received because there is something wrong in our lives, which needs to be put right. But this can get twisted into a continual searching for the key to unlock the door into the Father's presence. All sorts of strange things are unearthed to be repented of or broken in our lives in order to release the blessings we seek.

Satan will take advantage of this and remind you of things long dealt with, and try to convince you that they are still a problem. This can cause guilt and condemnation in lives where there should be none.

> *There is now no condemnation for those who are in Christ Jesus." (Rom.8:1)*

There is also a danger which comes from such teaching as the Word-Faith movement, which suggests that the power of our faith brings about the things we pray for. This means that if we don't receive what we pray for, then we don't have enough faith. This is devastating to those who pray earnestly and sincerely, and do not receive. Hudson Taylor once said, "We do not need a great faith, but faith in a great God."

> *When you pray, go into your room, close the door and pray to your Father, who is unseen. Then your Father, who sees what is done in secret, will reward you. (Matt.6:6)*

> *After Jesus had gone indoors, his disciples asked him privately, "Why couldn't we drive it out?" He replied, "This kind can come out only by prayer and fasting." (Mark 9:28-29)*

It is also true that sometimes specific instructions are given as to what should be done in a particular situation. But this too can get twisted, and the belief grows up that there is only one right way to do anything spiritual, and if this is not followed then it will not be effective.

God wants you to be honest in your relationship with him, sincere in your desires, and humbly willing to be used for his purposes. He has promised to *"give you the desires of your heart" (Ps.37:4)*. And he has spoken out against ritual observances and empty words.

> *Some have wandered away from these and turned to meaningless talk. They want to be teachers of*

*the law, but they do not know what they are
talking about or what they so confidently affirm.
(1 Tim.1:6,7)*

When the phenomenon of the Toronto Blessing broke,
church leaders and others rushed there to see what they
were doing that made them so effective. Then they
returned to their churches and implemented the same
things: pushing people to make sure they fell down,
praying over people's feet until they started shaking,
and so on. Any genuine benefit was sometimes lost in
trying for the special techniques that would work.

The Solution

If you have a piece of equipment which is old and
doesn't work properly, you try to repair it. But if it's
new and doesn't work properly, you send it back to the
manufacturer. Jesus is *"the author and perfecter of our
faith" (Heb.12:2).* If there is something wrong with
your faith, send it back to him who gave it to you and
let him put it right. The same verse says *"Let us fix our
eyes on Jesus".*

> *I know whom I have believed, and am convinced
> that he is able... (2 Tim.1:12)*

There are many reasons why God may not appear to
respond to us. Sometimes we are simply too impatient.

Sometimes we are not open minded enough to see that the answer may not be in the form we expected. Sometimes God knows better than we do what we need. Perhaps what we need is patience or trust!

> *What then shall we say? Is God unjust? Not at all! For he says to Moses, "I will have mercy on whom I have mercy, and I will have compassion on whom I have compassion."*
> *It does not, therefore, depend on man's desire or effort, but on God's mercy. (Rom.9:14-16)*

That wonderful lady, Corrie Ten Boom, expressed our need to trust God and his plans for us, in this poem:

My life is but a weaving, between my God and me
I do not choose the colours, He worketh steadily.
Oftimes He weaveth sorrow, and I in foolish pride,
Forget He sees the upper, and I the underside.

Not till the loom is silent and the shuttles cease to fly
Will God unroll the canvas and explain the reason why,
The dark threads are as needful in the skillful Weaver's hand,
As the threads of gold and silver in the pattern He has planned.

If you really want a magic formula to improve your relationship with God, try this one:

> *Let the word of God dwell in you richly...*
> *(Col.3:16)*

The Scriptures will make plain to you what is to many

people a mystery. They cannot see how anyone can have the power to be obedient to God's commands, to walk in his ways, and to be acceptable in his sight. The mystery is a secret no longer:

> *...God has chosen to make known... the glorious riches of this mystery, which is Christ in you, the hope of glory. (Col.1:27)*

Because we have Christ in us, we no longer have to rely on our own strength. Paul told the Ephesians that God has:

> *...made us alive with Christ...*
> *...seated us with him in the heavenly realms...*
> and prayed that they would be enlightened to
> understand *"...his incomparably great power for us who believe." (Eph.2:5,6; 1:19)*

And Peter wrote that

> *His divine power has given us everything we need for life and godliness... (2 Pet.1:3)*

ANSWERS TO EVERYTHING

The Truth

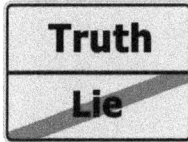

As Christians we seek to live our lives according to the word of God. When we search the Scriptures we find that there are some topics on which the Bible is very clear and some on which we can make decisions based on Biblical principles. However, we also find that on some topics the Bible is either unclear or totally silent.

The same is true of direct spiritual guidance and answers to prayer. Sometimes we know with startling clarity, sometimes we are guessing, and sometimes there are no answers at all. And often, guidance and understanding are hardest to find when we need them most. These are difficult issues which we all have to face.

For we know in part and we prophesy in part; but when perfection comes, the imperfect disappears... Now we see but a poor reflection as in a mirror; then we shall see face to face. Now I know in part; then shall I know fully, even as I am fully known. (1 Cor.13:9,10,12)

The truth is that God is sovereign, and does not reveal all of his plan to us.

For my thoughts are not your thoughts, neither are your ways my ways, declares the Lord. As the heavens are higher than the earth, so are my ways higher than your ways and my thoughts than your thoughts. (Isa.55:8-9)

The Trap

One of the attractions of many cults is that they offer an answer to everything – every question you may have about God and his purposes, and where you fit in. A precise interpretation for every passage in the Bible, even the irrelevant ones. A complete set of beliefs covering every eventuality. It can be a comforting thought to have no uncertainty, to know exactly what to believe about everything. Unfortunately, many of their answers are wrong.

Which is it better to have, no answer or any answer?

The cults would seem to prefer the latter, and come up with all sorts of contortions to explain every tiny point. The comfort of knowing there is always an answer can become the restriction of always checking out what you think you believe with the 'party line'. You can lose the ability to think for yourself.

If you look for a rigidly defined set of beliefs you are heading back to the law, and will soon find them a straitjacket rather than a comfort.

The Solution

Since the Christian faith is about relationships rather than dogma, there are bound to be areas which are not clear-cut. It takes maturity in our faith to accept the fact that there are many things we do not understand.

Immature faith is like the child who continually says "Why?" The child may ask "Why is the sky blue?", and we know there is a scientific explanation, but it is far beyond the ability of the child to understand, perhaps beyond our ability too. Yet we cannot accept that we may be in the same position regarding the things we do not understand on a spiritual level.

Part of our faith in God is that he can be trusted, even when we don't understand. It is only necessary that we know him. We all have to work on our own relationship with him, which will differ in some respects because we are different people with different needs.

It is worth quoting Hudson Taylor again here: "We do not need a great faith, but faith in a great God." This trust is vital in guiding our lives according to his will.

> *I know whom I have believed, and am convinced that he is able to guard what I have entrusted to him for that day. (2 Tim.1:12)*

SCRIPTURE TWISTING

The Truth

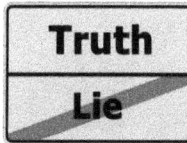

As a Christian the Bible means a lot to me. It has been my companion for years. I have learned that its words are God's Word, its commands his will, its perspective on life the only true one. Of course, it has puzzled me with its enigmas and the depth of its insight. I am often frustrated by what I believe God is demanding of me through the words on its pages. it encourages me, but it breaks me. It thrills me and it frightens me.

> *"But one thing it does not do: it does not come to me in such a way that I can pick and choose what to hold as true or false. As a Christian I find myself under its authority." (*Scripture Twisting *by James W. Sire, p.10)*

> *All Scripture is God-breathed and is useful for teaching, rebuking, correcting, and training in righteousness, so that the man of God may be*

thoroughly equipped for every good work. (2 Tim.3:16-17)

Jesus told his followers to search the Scriptures, and this is a key element in the life of a Christian. Within their pages is the word of God and the truths of the gospel. But the Bible is not like an instruction manual, with everything set out plainly in logical order. We must be careful in the way we interpret what we read.

The Trap

[Paul's] letters contain some things that are hard to understand, which ignorant and unstable people distort, as they do the other Scriptures, to their own destruction. Therefore, dear friends, since you already know this, be on your guard so that you may not be carried away by the error of lawless men and fall from your secure position. (2 Peter 2:16-17 RSV)

The Scriptures can be twisted in many ways. The cults do it deliberately in order to use the authority of the Bible to reinforce their claims. But even Christians can fall into the trap of misunderstanding or reading things into the Scriptures that are not really there. Many errors have crept into the church in the past because of this. For example, it took Martin Luther to make a stand before the teaching of grace was finally accepted, even though it seems plain to us today.

By ignoring context and picking up bits of Scripture, it is possible to prove almost anything from the Bible. For example, *"There is no God." (Ps.14:1).*

Here are just a few of the ways in which Scripture can be twisted:

1. Ignoring context

This is especially dangerous in the practice of opening the Bible at random and lighting on a verse for guidance, but it can also appear to support teaching which is incorrect. For example:

> *Then Peter came to Jesus and asked, "Lord, how many times shall I forgive my brother when he sins against me? Up to seven times?" Jesus answered, "I tell you, not seven times, but seventy-seven times." (Matt.18:21-22).*

This verse has been used to prevent people from speaking out when they are being hurt or misused by other Christians, or even by their leaders. They are accused of having an unforgiving spirit and made to feel guilty because they can't or won't forgive.

Looking at the context of this passage, the chapter begins with the disciples' question, *"Who then is the greatest in the kingdom of heaven?"* and ends with the parable of the unforgiving servant. Because of his unforgiveness, the king *"handed him over to the torturers until he should repay all that was owed him."* The final verse contains Jesus' warning, *"So shall my* *heavenly Father also do to you, if each of you does not forgive his brother, **from your heart**.*"

Peter is searching for a formula for how to be the greatest in the kingdom of heaven, but once again, as in so many places in Scripture, Jesus points out that God's standards are beyond our reach. It is not a question of how many times we forgive, but the kind of forgiveness. He who cannot forgive from the heart will find himself handed over to the torturers.

Such forgiveness is beyond us, in truth. It is only when we realise our inadequacy that we can turn to the source of our righteousness for the strength to obey. Our only hope is in God's mercy. The emphasis is on integrity, purity of heart, rather than covering up.

It is also interesting to note that in Luke 17:3 we are told *"Be on your guard! If your brother sins, rebuke him; and **if he repents** forgive him."* Is this saying that our forgiveness should be conditional? Does God forgive those who do not repent? Let us at least say that releasing someone from our vengeance does not mean that we should trust them or associate with them again, and certainly does not mean we should keep quiet about sin.

2. Putting together separate Scriptures which do not belong.

For example: 1 Cor.15:31 *"I die daily"* and Matt.16:24 *"Then Jesus said to his disciples, 'If anyone wishes to come after me, let him deny himself, and take up his cross, and follow me.'"*

These verses are used on the subject of self-denial.
They are used to say that we must do away with every
thought for ourselves and shoulder the burdens of what
God wants us to do. This can lead away from grace and
back to works.

1 Cor.15:31 is in the context of a discussion on the
resurrection, not self-denial. Having established the
truth of the resurrection, Paul asks *"why do we
endanger ourselves every hour?"*, and he ends the
chapter with the exhortation *"stand firm. Let nothing
move you."* Paul is saying that because of his
confidence in being raised from the dead he feels free
to put his life at risk for the sake of the gospel.

In Matt.16:24 the cross we must take up is the cross of
Christ.

> *For whoever wants to save his life will lose it, but
> whoever loses his life for me will find it... Or
> what can a man give in exchange for his soul?
> (Matt.16:25,26)*

There is no service or sacrifice we can give that will
merit us anything in seeking salvation. Self-denial, if
you want to call it that, is denying that there is anything
that we ourselves can do to merit eternal life, and
looking to Christ.

Not only do these verses not teach what they are being
used for, but they are not even about the same subject.

Illustrating points 1 & 2 together is the amusing story

of the lady who opened her Bible at random for guidance and came upon the verse *"And Judas went out and hanged himself."* (Matt.27:5). Finding this unhelpful she tried again, and found *"Go and do likewise."* (Luke 10:37). Such are the dangers of ignoring context and putting together Scriptures which do not belong!

3. Misquotation

Especially when we quote from memory, it is easy to be inaccurate. A classic misquotation is "Money is the root of all evil." The actual verse *says "For the love of money..."* (1 Tim.6:10). This is not as harmless as you might think. It would make quite a sermon on the value of poverty, particularly if the object was to persuade you to give up all your evil money to the speaker's church or pet cause!

4. Selective attention to Scripture

This is choosing the parts that fit our way of thinking without reference to the whole message. This is very similar to ignoring context, but on a wider scale. Whole theologies can be built on a range of Scriptures which sound very plausible when you are listening to the sermon, but do not check out with the wider message of the books from which they come, or indeed with the Bible as a whole.

For example I once heard a well-respected Christian leader quote *"All these people were still living by faith when they died"* (Heb.11:13), and use it to teach that if we do not test our faith every day we could find we were saved yesterday but not today. The verse continues *"They did not receive the things promised, they only saw them and welcomed them from a distance."* The writer to the Hebrews is saying that they trusted God, even though they had not seen their salvation. That is why they were still living by faith, not for fear of losing their salvation.

This is a technique known as proof-texting, which is forming an opinion in your own mind and then looking for a Scripture to back up what you have already decided. This is very dangerous and cultic thinking. The correct approach is to come to Scripture with an open mind, research all that it has to say on the subject, and then reason out what the message is, even if we do not like the answer.

The Solution

It is vital that we use sound principles in our attempts to understand the Bible.

- Look at each Scripture, not only in the context of the immediate surrounding verses, but of the book from which it comes, and the teaching of the Bible as a whole. For example, James 2:14-26 appears to teach salvation by works. However, this does not fit with the rest of the New Testament, which clearly teaches *"not by works, so that no-one can boast"* (Eph.2:9). In the past it was suggested that James and Paul disagreed with one another, and that the book of James should not even be in the Bible! However, a closer reading of the passage shows that James is asking *"Can such faith save him?"* As shown earlier, James is saying that the works are produced by the kind of faith which saves.

- Consider whether this is a piece of advice for a specific situation or time, or whether it can be applied in a wider context and is still relevant today. For example, Paul's advice to slaves and masters (Eph.6:5-9, Col.3:22-4:1). Such teaching does not condone slavery, but was given by God as practical ways of dealing with the realities of the day.
- Consider the original audience for the Scripture. Sometimes we have to view Scriptures through the culture of its time, for example the passage in 1 Cor.11:5-6 about women covering their hair and not shaving their heads. In the culture of the time, uncovered hair was a sign of loose morals in a woman, and a woman's head was shaved because she had either been publicly disgraced or was in rebellion against her husband. These things do not apply today in our culture, although the underlying ideas about modesty and marriage do.

We need to be familiar with Scripture and the truths of the gospel which it teaches. Jesus condemned the religious leaders of his day for their lack of understanding.

> *But Jesus answered them, "You are wrong, because you know neither the Scriptures nor the power of God." (Matt.22:29)*

Studying the Scriptures will enable us to be alert to teaching which is suspect, and to be able to check out anything which does not ring true.

> *Do your best to present yourself to God as one approved, a workman who does not need to be ashamed and who correctly handles the word of truth. (2 Tim.2:15)*

SUPERSTITION

The Truth

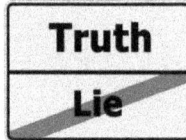

The early Christians met together in the temple courts and in their homes *(Acts 2:46-47)*. They held on to the promise that wherever two or three are gathered, Jesus would be there *(Matt.18:20)*. They did not need to have a special building in which to meet. They had no special ceremonies apart from baptism and the Lord's Supper.

> *Therefore do not let anyone judge you by what you eat or drink, or with regard to a religious festival, a New Moon celebration or a Sabbath day. These are a shadow of the things that were to come; the reality, however, is found in Christ. (Col.2:16-17)*

In the centuries since then, Christians have built their

own places of worship, into which has gone much loving care, as a token of their love for God. Rituals have developed with the intention of glorifying God and assisting us to worship him. We like to have pictures and items with Christian symbols to remind and encourage us, and in those countries where Christians are not persecuted, are proud to wear a cross or other symbol as a sign to others of our faith.

But all these things are only embellishments, and are not an essential part of our relationship with God. They remind, inspire, assist us, but we must not become dependent upon them.

Should we behave differently in certain places? Or should we be *"in Christ' at all times and in all places?" (Gal.2:20)*. Are certain places, times or objects endowed with special spiritual powers? Or can we be used by God and in touch with God anywhere? Cannot God see us everywhere and whatever we do?

The Trap

We condemn those who worship idols, and sacred places, yet we have made a whole set of rules about what we should wear and what we should do when we meet together. We are superstitious about our church buildings as 'The Lord's House'. God no longer needs a house, since he dwells in our hearts *(1 Cor.3:16)*.

There are many unwritten rules about dress and behaviour, which the visitor or new Christian can cross unknowingly. Criticism and disapproval can put someone off and drive them away. The important thing is that they come to church to learn the gospel and worship God, not how they dress. Young children can be unwelcome in services because they can be noisy and disruptive. This precludes their parents as well, thus preventing more people from coming to God.

Such superstitious behaviour has caused problems, for example, with those who come seeking Christ from unsavoury backgrounds. The tramp, the drug addict, the hooligan with no manners, are all turned away by our disapproval of their 'inappropriate' dress and behaviour in meetings. Jackie Pullinger, when she began to convert the drug addicts in Hong Kong, found them unwelcome in the local Christian churches, and was forced to start a church of her own—something she was against doing. And closer to home, those working with Teen Challenge in our own streets, find great difficulty in finding churches who will welcome the young people they reach.

The Sabbath day was ordained for man to rest, not as the special day on which to worship God. We are supposed to *"pray continually" (1 Thes.5:17)*, not just on Sundays.

There is nothing wrong in the wearing of a cross or sign of the fish, except when it is attributed with special powers to make the wearer feel safe or comforted. Being superstitious about this jewellery is akin to idol worship.

The Solution

It is good to show respect for our place of worship, and to show respect for God in the way we dress and act. But since we can do nothing to make God love us any more than he does already, these things must not be given special merit. We have already seen that God looks on our hearts, not on the outward appearance *(1 Sam.16:7)*. Love and tolerance in the beginning can help visitors come to know God and his love for them through you. As they and other new Christians grow in relationship with him they will desire to behave and dress more appropriately.

Those rituals and observances which help to focus our minds on God or help us in our obedience or our worship must not be elevated to the position of somehow essential to our salvation. Here we stray once again into legalism. We become upset and guilty if a ritual is omitted or disrupted.

For example, a daily quiet time is a discipline which can be a great blessing to us, and one we should do our best to follow. The problem comes when we are unavoidably unable to have our quiet time one day, or for several days, and feel guilty or insecure in our standing before God. Or when we become harsh with children or others who disrupt us for good reason, because we feel the day is spoiled without it.

Many of us are not even aware of the whole range of superstitions which have grown up in our own lives or in our congregations. The next time you are faced with something which seems inappropriate or disrespectful to God, stop and ask yourself, in the light of God's unconditional love and care for his people, if it really matters.

ELITISM

The Truth

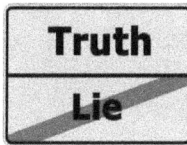

*You are all sons of God through faith in Christ
Jesus, for all of you who were baptised into
Christ have clothed yourselves with Christ. There
is neither Jew nor Greek, slave nor free, male nor
female, for you are all one in Christ Jesus.
(Gal.3:26-28)*

There is a great diversity in Christianity: different styles
of worship, formal and less formal services, different
emphases on the gifts and equipping of the Holy Spirit.
In this we should rejoice. God does not require us all to
fit into one mould. The famous passage in 1 Cor.12
reminds us that the body has many parts which all
function differently and are all essential. We are all
given the opportunity to find the place which God has
for us: the congregation where we feel most

comfortable and the work within that congregation that he wants us to fulfil.

The Trap

There are only two kinds of people in the world: those who are saved and those who are not. This may seem a very obvious thing to say, but there is creeping into the church the idea that, to paraphrase George Orwell, "*All Christians are equal, but some are more equal than others.*"

In some places people are frowned upon because they do not dress smartly to go to church. In others they are laughed at because they wear a suit and tie and everyone else is in jeans. In more formal churches, laughter or applause is considered inappropriate and disrespectful, and many are unhappy about demonstrative worship. On the other hand, those churches where people are demonstrative can be concerned about members who do not wave their hands or dance, but prefer to be quiet before God.

There is also elitism between congregations over these and other things. This is most marked in the area of the Holy Spirit. The charismatic movement has brought a reawakening of the life of the Spirit flowing in the lives of Christians and through their congregations. Faith has been deepened and become more dynamic. Theology is no longer theoretical. People believe that we can claim

God's promises today, and are realising that receiving Christ includes receiving the Spirit and his power in order to come into the full riches of God's kingdom living.

Unfortunately this has resulted in an elitism between what are seen as the 'haves' and the 'have nots'.

> *Claiming to be superior and to have arrived, they are often cruelly condemning in their attitude to others and refuse to take advice from anyone who is not of their own type of spirituality. This often springs not from any particularly vicious spiritual pride, but from false teaching to which they have been introduced on the subject of initiation, seeing it as necessarily a two-stage affair; other Christians may have reached stage one, but they have, through a 'baptism in the Holy Spirit' attained ipso facto to stage two—a mountain ridge from which they are unable to descend whatever they do (for they are Spirit-filled folk; they have arrived), a mountain ridge which relieves them of any further necessity to go on climbing.*
> *(I Believe In The Holy Spirit, Michael Green, p.264)*

Another area is the matter of communion. I have been in churches where members are served communion in trays where they sit, churches where members come to the front and kneel to receive communion from the minister, and churches where members come and help themselves and then share with one another. Let us not consider one way better than another, but be grateful for the service of communion.

The Solution

The Bible teaches us that all Christians have the Spirit.

> *For we were all baptised by one Spirit into one body... and we were all given the one Spirit to drink. (1 Cor.12:13)*

Indeed, it is the Spirit which lives in us which makes us Christians.

> *You, however, are controlled not by the sinful nature, but by the Spirit, if the Spirit of God lives in you, and if anyone does not have the Spirit of Christ, he does not belong to Christ. (Rom.8:9)*

The problem is that so many Christians do not know the overwhelming power of the Spirit manifest in their lives, and when they experience it, they feel as if they never had the Spirit before. Michael Green quotes from the Catholic writer Fr. Killian McDonnell, O.S.B.:

> *Hence, many prefer to use other expressions to describe what is happening in the charismatic renewal. Among other alternatives which have been proposed are: "release of the Spirit", "renewal of the sacraments of initiation",*

"actualisation of gifts already received in potentiality", and "a manifestation of baptism, whereby the hidden grace given in baptism breaks through into conscious experience". These are all ways of saying that the power of the Holy Spirit, given in Christian initiation, but hitherto unexperienced, becomes a matter of personal conscious experience.
(I Believe in the Holy Spirit, Michael Green, pp.176-7)

We should not be satisfied with a low level of spirituality, and should encourage all to allow God to release them into deeper experiences. We must ensure that Christian initiation is the full New Testament concept, including *"the water and the Spirit"* (John 3:5). But let us not divide the church and accuse others of not being Christians because they are not experiencing the fullness of what God has for them.

> *Then you will not take pride in one man over against another. For who makes you different from anyone else? What do you have that you did not receive? And if you did receive it, why do you boast as though you did not? (1 Cor.4:6b-7)*

In the same way, Christians with different worship styles or dress codes must look beyond the superficial and welcome one another as brothers in Christ.

> *So, if you think you are standing firm, be careful that you don't fall! (1 Cor.10:12)*

> *When someone invites you to a wedding feast, do*

not take the place of honour... But when you are invited, take the lowest place, so that when your host comes he will say to you, 'Friend, move up to a better place.' Then you will be honoured in the presence of all your fellow guests. For everyone who exalts himself will be humbled, and he who humbles himself will be exalted. (Luke 14:8-11)

THE NEED TO SEE

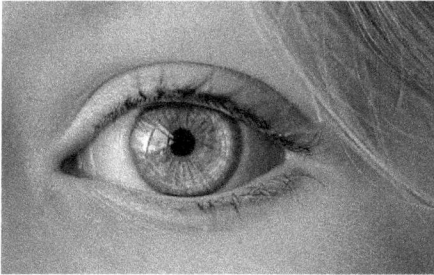

The Truth

God has promised he will answer our prayers, but he
has not promised what his answer will be. It can be
hard to wait and not to know. Although we read in the
Bible, and in the lives of Christians throughout the
ages, accounts of God moving in a supernatural way –
visions, voices, miracles – these occasions are rare.
God will fulfil his purposes, and sometimes he does so
in a spectacular way, but mostly it is done quietly and
often unnoticed. The Psalms are full of cries that God
appears to have turned away, leaving them to trust in
faith that he has not forgotten them.

> *Faith is being sure of what we hope for and
> certain of what we do not see. (Hebrews 11:1)*

In the film *The Golden Compass*, of the book by Philip

Pulman, Lyra has an alethiometer with which she communicates with the 'dust' – the essence of all life. When she asks a question, the hands move to point to symbols, through which the answer is revealed to her. How we would love to have some way of telling us God's answers to our prayers! But God tells us that his ways and thoughts are higher than ours *(Isaiah 55:8)*. We cannot grasp his infinite plans, and must trust what we do not understand.

Peter promised us that *"His divine power has given us everything we need for life and godliness." (1 Peter 1:3).* There will be times when the way is clear and times when our hearts soar with the touch of the Holy Spirit, but these are times of special blessing, not our everyday experience. Do not let people make you feel inadequate because you do not live your life 'on the mountain top'.

The Trap

The Bible says "*a wicked and adulterous generation seeks after a sign.*" (Luke 11:29). Although most of us would not consider ourselves 'wicked and adulterous,' deep in our hearts we all need to see evidence that things are true. When we pray, so often there is no instant response.

The attraction of the Toronto Blessing and similar

manifestations is that, when you pray for someone, they fall over. Here is evidence that your prayer is working. Or if you are the one prayed for, the spiritual feeling that sweeps over you and takes your strength gives you assurance that God is indeed moving and responding. Yet, how often does this happen and the prayer is not ultimately answered in the affirmative? At the height of the Toronto Blessing I saw a young couple who were living together outside marriage fall down under prayer and get up with radiant faces – and then go home and carry on as before, unchanged. If God truly moves in your life, the experience will change you.

The Solution

The wonderful thing about Christianity is that God's promises are written down, so we can be sure of them. We do not need to see instant results or signs to know that he is faithful to his promises.

> *The Lord is faithful to all his promises and loving to all he has made. (Psalm 145:13b)*

Spend more time studying these promises and remember the times in the past when God has answered your prayers and those of others, and especially where things have worked out very differently to what you hoped for, but were still for your benefit.

If you have been living with 'the need to see', it can be hard to let go. Life can seem uncertain and unsafe. You need to retrain yourself away from this and get back to the solid foundations of promises whose outcome you cannot see, but you can believe in.

As a simple example, many years ago, when I moved from a very charismatic church to a more formal one, I found it hard to worship without getting excited and jumping around and getting a 'buzz'. One day in church I clearly felt the message "*Their worship is just as acceptable to me.*" I was reminded of the Scripture that man looks on the outward appearance, but God looks on the heart, and looked at the hearts of those in church around me and realised that truth. It was a growing experience for me to learn to worship God in stillness too.

In the Truth part of this topic I mentioned that the Psalms are full of cries that God seems to have turned away, leaving them to trust in his promises. Here are some of their responses. May your life respond in this way too.

> *My soul faints with longing for your salvation, but I have put my hope in your word. (Psalm 119:81)*

> *Your promises have been thoroughly tested, and your servant loves them… Trouble and distress have come upon me, but your commands are my delight. (Psalm 119:140, 143)*

CONCLUSION

In the section on the trap of Legalism, we spoke of how we very often apply the wrong medicine in trying to put our lives right before God. Let us look at what is the right medicine.

We apply the wrong medicine because we do not remember who we really are in Christ. God has said things about you that you need to know, that you need to build into your understanding, and there are some things you need to do in the light of them.

The early Christians devoted themselves to the apostles teaching *(Acts 2:42)*. The amount you understand about what God has done for you and in you, makes a difference. There is something about the presence of God that changes us. There is a releasing power that answers many of the problems that you face day by day.

Paul felt that knowing Christ was the most precious thing in life:

> *But whatever was to my profit I now consider loss for the sake of Christ. What is more, I consider everything a loss compared to the surpassing greatness of knowing Christ Jesus my Lord, for whose sake I have lost all things. I consider them rubbish, that I may gain Christ and be found in him, not having a righteousness of my own that comes from the law, but that which is through faith in Christ--the righteousness that comes from God and is by faith. (Phil.3:7-9)*

But this must be more than head knowledge, more than intellectual understanding. These truths must be built into us so as to affect the way we think and feel. Once these things become real to us, our whole perspective changes.

We must be wary of our leaders too, and not follow blindly. Paul warned us *'test everything; hold fast what is good.' (1 Thes 5.21)* and that includes our church leaders and those we allow to influence us.

> *And Jesus answered them, "See that no one leads you astray...*
> *For false christs and false prophets will arise and perform great signs and wonders, so as to lead astray, if possible, even the elect." (Matt 24.4 & 24)*
> *Beloved, do not believe every spirit, but test the spirits to see whether they are from God, for many false prophets have gone out into the world. (1 John 4.1)*

We need to look into the mirror of God's Word and see what we really are, and not forget when we go away from it *(James 1:23-25)*. Try reading Romans chapters 6, 7 & 8. Here are just some of the truths about us:

- ..our old self was crucified with him... anyone who has died has been freed from sin (6:6-7)
- ..sin shall not be your master (6:14)
- ..set free from sin (6:18)
- ..released from the law (7:6)
- ..no condemnation (8:1)
- ..controlled not by the sinful nature but by the Spirit (8:9)
- ..sons of God... God's children... heirs of God and co-heirs with Christ (8:14-17)
- ..called... justified... glorified (8:30)

Jesus said:

I am the vine; you are the branches. If a man remains in me and I in him, he will bear much fruit; apart from me you can do nothing. (John 15:5)

and the Psalmist said:

He is like a tree planted by streams of water, which yields its fruit in season and whose leaf does not wither. (Ps.1:3)

Branches do not strain to bear fruit, it is a natural result of the life they draw from the roots. We have no need to look any further than the work Christ has already done for us. We have no need for special keys to unlock the blessings of God.

His divine power has given us everything we need for life and godliness through our knowledge of him who called us by his own glory and goodness. (2 Peter 1:3)

Maturity and liberty comes from knowing God, knowing what God has done for us and living resolutely in the light of it and being totally committed to it. Not moved in any shape, form or way from the truth that is in the gospel.

###

Thank you for reading this book. I hope you enjoyed it.

Reviews are an author's lifeblood. If you enjoyed this book, please go online to Amazon and leave a review. It doesn't have to be long.

Ann M Thomas

OTHER BOOKS BY THIS AUTHOR

Medieval History
Alina, the White Lady of Oystermouth
Broken Reed: The Lords of Gower and King John
The Magna Carta: The Layman's Guide to the Great Charter
Medieval Gower Stories
Swansea Miracle (coming 2021)

Science Fiction
Intruders, Flight of the Kestrel book 1
Alien Secrets, Flight of the Kestrel book 2
Crisis of Conscience, Flight of the Kestrel book 3
and look out for Planet Fail, Flight of the Kestrel book 4

Poetry
My Stroke of Inspiration

FREE BOOK!
Join the author's mailing list and receive these free
books and monthly updates http://eepurl.com/bbOsyz

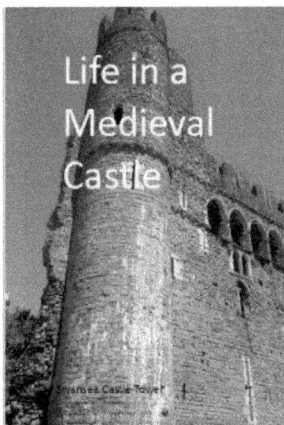